MANAGING THE BOOK ON YOU!

YOU!

Rewriting Your Leadership Story

Dr. Lalia Rach

ISBN: 979-8-9866914-0-4 (Paperback)

Library of Congress Control Number: 2022914220

For permission requests or for information about special discounts available for bulk purchases, sales promotions, fund-raising and educational needs contact:

Printed in the United States of America

Lalia Rach, Ed.D.
Founder and Partner
Rach Enterprises

Websites:

www.rachenterprises.com

www.alhi.com

LinkedIn:

www.linkedin.com/in/laliarach

Emails:

laliarach@rachenterprises.com

lalia@alhi.com

For Jan, always and forever

Table of Contents

What Leaders are Saying

A must read filled with experience and humor. You know you really like a book when you've turned the last page and you want to keep reading and thinking. This book is Leadership gold; a deceptively straightforward playbook filled with experience and passion. It provides a roadmap to assess your development that can be continually revisited in your quest to be the leader you want to be.
Suzanne Hillman, President & CEO, Southern Management Companies

---

What I most enjoyed about the book was that it was a workbook with specific exercises to complete. It challenged me to think and then put actions in place to improve my leadership skills.
Peter Strebel, Chairman, Omni Hotels & Resorts

Lalia Rach uses her collective experience to curate the questions needed for women's professional growth and self-awareness. This book is a tool that women can revisit as they move through their leadership trajectory.
Allison Kinsley, CMM, CMP, CED, Chief Meeting Architect, Kinsley Meetings

---

I wish I had this book 20 years ago for my younger self as the stories, advice and workbook are an extraordinary way to explore understanding who you are and what you've become. The workbook is straightforward, and engaging and allowed me to reflect a ton. Kudos to Lalia for taking a step beyond existing leadership books out there today. This book and workbook are very effective! In this book, Lalia has a wonderful style to help guide anyone wanting to learn, grow and develop.

Melissa Maher, Senior marketing leader in Travel & Technology, most recently: B2B Chief Marketing Officer & SVP Marketing & Industry Engagement, Expedia

---

This book is overflowing with fundamental lessons on how to be a better, more well-rounded, more thoughtful leader. Lalia breaks it down as only she can into thought-provoking, tangible exercises that allow the reader to explore a framework for leadership and beyond, tapping into a process akin to her "uncommon sense" approach that encourages the reader to think outside the box. I will be sharing this book with colleagues and emerging leaders and revisiting it myself as a guide on leadership and humanity.

Marina MacDonald, Chief Marketing Officer, Red Roof Corporate Headquarters

---

This book is a must read for women professionals. It is having a personal coach help you self-chart your career development. It asks the tough questions and helps you build personal accountability in owning your journey. Lalia's blend of personal storytelling and practical career advice is relatable, authentic and is a source of truth. Thank you, Lalia, for being such a great advocate for women leaders and for telling leadership stories that we all need to hear.

Dorothy Dowling, C Suite Marketing and Commercial Leader, Public Board Director. Formerly Chief Marketing Officer & SVP, BWH Hotel Group

---

For the 25 years I have known Lalia, I've seen her approach her work in a variety of situations. This book reflects who she is as a professional and a leader. She has written a practical and useful book to assist anyone in becoming a better leader. Her voice is authentic, and her stories bring the leadership ideas to life.

Jonathan Tisch, Chairman and CEO, Loews Hotels & Co., Co-owner New York Giants Football Team

---

Lalia does it all! Over the years she has been my executive coach, coached several of my team members, led our town hall meetings and brand conference panels and discussions, and most importantly, she has been an honest friend, who always tells it like she sees it. Her straightforward, no-nonsense approach is on full display in her book as she offers practical advice along with real-world examples an important read and resource for all leaders.

Andrew Alexander, CEO, Green Courte Residential Holdings

When I started reading the book, the thought did cross my mind that this book might not be for me, however, it was at that moment, that I thought, this book can help me from two different angles. First, to help me be an even better me. The stories, regardless of who they are from, are a very good way to get a person to open up, reflect, and relate. The book also can help me be a better leader/coach. It serves as a great reminder that we all have our own stories and situational/servant leadership is needed (more now so than ever). This workbook will help me in coaching my team. It gives me some great questions to work into my conversations.
Jeff Bzdawka, Chief Executive Officer, Knowland

Kudos to Dr. Rach on crafting a unique and practical approach to personal and professional development, rooted on a foundation of self-evaluation, personal accountability and action. If you aspire to be a stronger leader, invaluable colleague and to dramatically transform others' perceptions of you, then completing Lalia's workbook is a great start.
Paul Van Deventer, President and CEO Meeting Planners Informational

---

Acknowledgments

Acknowledging the guidance and advice from others is a daunting and fulfilling task. The daunting part includes fear of forgetting someone and of sounding like a sycophant. The fulfilling aspect comes from the joy of realizing how wonderful life is when those who love you care enough to read a near-final draft and think well of what you have done. Hearing back from those I asked to be a reader was a bit of a Sally Field moment for me: "I can't deny the fact that you like me. Right now, you like me." Only for me it was you love me!

My thanks to Donna Quadri-Felletti, Ph.D., Margo Wood, Marti Wiener and Fran Johnson for reading and offering feedback. Each of you is a valued friend, colleague, and someone I rely upon when I lose my way or become a champion complainer. This book is better because of you.

Life is filled with unexpected turns, and one happened on a summer's day in 2021 after I moved back to Madison, WI for yet the fourth time and met our new neighbors. One neighbor, having had a multifaceted career in library science and upon leaving full-time work, became a book coach. Now mind you I really didn't know I should have a book coach but as I listened to what she did and how she helped so many people become authors I knew the universe was handing me an unexpected opportunity on a silver platter! Mary Helen Conroy is a best-selling author and *my* book coach. She is a person who knew just the right buttons to push and words to say to keep me going. You are a joy and so good at what you do. I'm singing the Golden Girls introduction song in my head as I write this. Thank you for being my coach!

Mary Helen introduced me to my book editor, Ann Massie Nelson. Ann provided a deft touch directing change that improved the overall readability of my writing.

So many of the professionals I have coached over the past few decades encouraged me when I shared I was writing a book. Not only are you a part of this book but unbeknownst gave me inspiration when sorely needed. While my stories are not about one of you in particular, I am confident you will be reminded of my words when you read the book.

I am fortunate to call many professionals colleague and friend. While I cannot mention all, I must acknowledge the support and belief of Mike Dominguez, CEO of Associated Luxury Hotels International. Mike, you never questioned that I could write a book on leadership, you only offered encouragement. I am grateful for this and for the relationship we have developed over the years. How we met is a story for another book, but the happenstance of the meeting has turned into one of the most meaningful relationships of my professional life.

My last acknowledgment is Jan Hatleberg. Her sense of humor, eye for detail and intellectual capabilities consistently entertain and amaze me. Her belief in my abilities is breathtaking and glorious. She never doubted that I could do this, she never wavered in her kindness toward me when I ranted and raved at my inability to string two sentences together during a long siege of writer's block. Thank you, Jan, for believing even when I did not.

Introduction

Why write a self-guided workbook for executives when the proverbial bookshelves are overflowing with volumes on how to become a better or more complete executive, with each promising a different take on what is holding you back? Short answer, I believe there is an element of professional development that has been overlooked or underappreciated as vital to continued professional success. That vital element is making certain that who you have become and what you have changed is clearly understood by those you work with, hence, Managing the Book on You.

I have coached many executives over the past three decades, mainly women in mid- and senior-level positions in Fortune 500 corporations, family-owned businesses and everything in between. While the focus of my coaching is on assisting the professional in becoming a better leader, it became clear that it wasn't enough for the individual to improve and grow. They needed to actively change the out-of-date views and assumptions held about them by colleagues, bosses and team members.

I had an ah-ha moment in late 2019 while coaching an executive vice president of a hospitality company. As I explained a way to view what she was experiencing, I asked her to consider if colleagues recognized how she had changed in the 20-odd years she had been working for the same company. I asked her to describe herself as a 20-something associate and to contrast and compare it to the 40-something executive she is today. She had an impressive list of tangible accomplishments, had worked to improve her executive presence and emotional maturity and was now engaging a coach to navigate what she called the "finishing touches." This was a reasonable approach but as she compared her development, I realized yet again that a client had not focused on "telling and showing" others just who she had become as a professional and a leader.

I began to talk about what I viewed as the missing element: She needed to actively revise and update how others viewed her. I characterized it as editing the book others wrote about her. She had to actively manage the small and large impressions held by her boss that were no longer valid. She needed to address views her colleagues had of her from some time ago as these views could be kept alive because a colleague was threatened by the change the professional represented. I offered a few questions for her to think about. When she was less experienced, was she a micro-manager? Too much of a people pleaser? Unwilling to have direct conversations about difficult issues? Someone who made mountains out of molehills? Was she seen as too aggressive?

As we worked through these and additional aspects of her younger, less experienced version of leadership, I explained why understanding who you are—and who you've become—matters. My client asked me why I hadn't written a book about my approach. That question stopped me in my tracks. As someone who is seldom at a loss for words, I was. Her question made me realize writing a book about "managing the book on you" was something I could and should do.

This book is more than stories and advice. It is a workbook, a place for you to explore the views, assumptions and beliefs others hold about you that are no longer current. Putting who you are into proper focus for others is something many of us ignore and pay the price for doing so. Throughout the book there will be examples to help you identify what you were versus what you have become. The narrative and workbook will help you identify opportunities for you to demonstrate what has changed about you.

- *What you were*:
  As a less experienced professional you may have been reticent about speaking up or disagreeing. You might have been viewed as having a lack of confidence or a desire not to rock the boat.
- *What you have become*:
  Tangible changes including promotions, certificates, associations you are active in, and improvements to your executive presence. Intangible changes include being more emotionally mature, a better listener, less inclined to jump to conclusions, and more collaborative.

As you progress through the book it will become yours, containing stories, phrases and characteristics that others have gathered about you and your leadership style. Your book will clearly detail your leadership development. The chapters can be revised and updated regularly to document your progress and will validate your growth to yourself and coworkers so that you are truly managing your book and the one others have written on you!

How to Use This Book

Each chapter starts with a quote that I believe intertwines with the written message. I love quotes and use them to anchor my thinking and to inspire and challenge me. I want my thinking to have a visceral and intellectual quality. Quotes help me accomplish this.

I write as I speak so if you are able to hear my voice throughout the book it may lead you to a deeper connection with the ideas and concepts.

Throughout the book there are pages to take notes, ask yourself a question, or indicate you need to reread a section. This is one way to make the book your own and to begin the process of rewriting your leadership story.

This book is intended to be easy to read, interesting and useful. It is in the useful intent that your hard work is required. Simply reading it is not enough. Oh, you can just read it but the return on your investment will be minimal as the return is found in answering the workbook questions located at the end of each chapter.

To do the work, to better *manage the book on you* I suggest the following process:

1.   Read and re-read the chapter. Think about what I am saying as you read. Use the right-hand margin to make notes. Did something resonate with you? Do you want to follow up on an idea, find additional information about a concept online or talk to a colleague about a point I made? Make this your book.

2.   Read the workbook questions. Consider what you need to do to answer them. Do you need to review other materials and take time to think, or do you need to talk to someone to gain insight? Take your time because answering the questions fully and thoughtfully matters.

3.   Set aside time to answer the questions. Some chapter questions may take an hour total, others a few weeks. There is no race to the finish as thinking clearly and honestly is what is needed. You need to analyze your reaction to ensure you get to the root of the matter.

4.   Do the work. Schedule the time. Be kind to yourself in your honesty. Reflect on what you learn. Know what you will do to improve, change and act.

It goes back to something we have all heard and know – what you put into it determines how much you get out of it. So, it's time to start Managing the Book on YOU.

Chapter 1

I don't see how (s)he can ever finish,

if (s)he doesn't begin.

Alice of *Alice in Wonderland*

−Lewis Carroll

Time to Begin

Key chapter points

- What to expect from this book
- Why managing the book on you matters
- How to compare your past you with the current you

As a professional, the way colleagues, employees and bosses view your leadership style is vital to your continued success. Too often this view is out of date reflecting who you *were* but not who you have *become*. As you actively work on improving as a leader, at the same time you must revise old thinking about you, your strengths and issues, your expectations and values. For example: It may have been as a less experienced professional you held yourself back in group meetings, did not speak up or disagree and did not sit at the table but took a chair out of the way.

Hopefully, this no longer applies as you have learned to engage more consistently and to sit at the table, but some colleagues may still hold earlier views of you as timid, hesitant or indecisive. This book is designed to assist you with changing long held beliefs about you and how others perceive your leadership abilities.

Many women I coach have greater credentials than their male counterparts. Framed and hung for all to see are certificates and diplomas for graduate degrees showing clearly the efforts taken to advance their knowledge base. Some women have served in acting or interim positions more than once, so their experience is deeper. Some waited longer for promotion as their company was slow to embrace a more diverse leadership structure.

Think about what you did when you earned a certificate, were elected to a professional association board seat, or were asked to participate in a conference general session panel. There may have been an internal memo announcing your accomplishment, a press release reporting your appointment, and a follow-up story in a professional magazine. There may be a plaque or picture you hung on the wall for visitors to see.

We readily update the tangible advances and changes to our resumes, yet the strides taken toward greater emotional maturity and improved leadership skills are not as easily shared. Can you imagine yourself exclaiming in a meeting, "I have worked for six months on my self-regulation and self-awareness skills!"

I have yet to see a certificate on the wall proclaiming one has improved as a listener, has become less emotional when under pressure, or consistently speaks in the declarative voice. Such skills evolve without an actual timeline but require definite commitment to learning new habits and behaviors that make us better professionals and leaders. Without a determined effort to inform others about your growth, it won't be noticed by those who define your professional reputation.

I will weave my own story throughout this book in an effort to ground your thinking and perhaps bring a smile or even a laugh. My journey is filled with detours, zero-to-60 moments, backups and hairpin turns. I view it as a series of local and long-distance trips to my destination as a professional and leader.

Your trip through my book should result in *your* book of stories, phrases and characteristics that others have gathered about you and your leadership style. It should give you a cohesive view of your leadership development that can be revised and added to regularly. To accomplish this you will need determination, commitment, desire and a sense of humor. Without these characteristics you can't adequately identify what you have changed and what you must continue to work on in your journey to advancing your career. But as Alice so wisely opined, if you don't begin it won't happen. Treat this book as something you must do - not something you would like to do.

A beginning story:

I remember as a child being told "practice makes perfect" by my mother. The reason for her urging was my lack of discipline when it came to practicing the piano or the cornet. To my thinking since I played both instruments by ear as I could not read music, practicing just didn't make sense. My musical career was short-lived as not being able to read music was a problem. I never produced the same song as the others in the band and my piano teacher thought I was just stubborn and not worth the aggravation. I avoided practicing because no matter what I tried I couldn't follow the notes on the page.

Similarly, was my experience in high school geometry. I mean, who cares what a trapezoid is or measures? My mind simply doesn't grasp the measurements of distance and space as normally taught. This challenge continued in college as courses on economics, accounting and statistics became my Waterloo and I actually received my first grade of F!

But rather than address the challenge I continued to avoid areas where I could not achieve perfection or find a workaround. I stopped putting in the effort to read music when I realized I would never be first chair cornet player. I didn't try to understand geometry, economics and abstract concepts since I would never be the best. Imagine my shock when my progress as an entry-level manager was threatened because I lacked basic financial and statistical knowledge.

That's when I realized I had to do more than talk a good game – I had to know how to lead the game! I came to grips with the fact I could learn about accounting and statistics, but I would never get an A. Once I dropped the rule that all that mattered was the A, I began to see that learning and understanding was the goal, not perfection.

Sharing my own challenge with various aspects of emotional intelligence is meant to assist you in dealing with your own. The guiding principle for anyone using this workbook is "you have to want to." I do not have the answers, but I am willing to think about my maturity issues and, while I am not always successful in my change, I know that I do slowly move toward my goal.

Chapter 1 Workbook

Time to Begin

Identify what you did *earlier* in your life or career when:

---

1. You avoided learning because it was too difficult.

2. How did this avoidance limit your career progress?

3. If the same things were to happen today, what would you do differently?

<u>Identify what you do *now*</u>:

1. What are three areas or topics you continue to avoid because they are too difficult?

2. How did this avoidance limit your career progress?

3. Identify the new skills have you mastered in the past three years.

Chapter 2

Don't get confused between

what people say you are

and who you know you are.

–Oprah Winfrey

Knowing Yourself as a Professional

Key chapter points

- Take a focused approach to clearly understand who you are as a professional
- Why spending time knowing yourself matters
- A simple but useful way of comparing who you think you are and who others think you are.

Understanding who you are is vital as a professional who leads people. When was the last time you honestly evaluated your professional strengths and challenges? It is time to be forthright about what you do well and where you need to improve. You need a realistic view of yourself if you are to contrast and compare what others say about you in a meaningful manner.

An honest self-assessment is a foundational action that should give you a clear indication of your professional maturity and informs what you need to work on to advance your abilities and skills. Do you readily accept what others think of you as a colleague or leader rather than weighing it against your own solid understanding of who you are? One way to determine this is to consider how important social media "likes" are to your overall self-esteem. Another is to reflect on how often you question your self-measure of a job well done and if you give more credit to someone else's opinion.

A commonality among the women I have coached is being far too self-effacing about their strengths — hemming and hawing, qualifying or parsing each statement so not to be boastful. I would remind them I was not asking for grandiose flights of fancy, just a simple declarative statement about their competency and skill. I urged them to categorize it as what they are good at and what gives them a sense of accomplishment and pride. Further guidelines were don't nitpick about "well I should be better at this one part" or "I would only give myself a 'B'." I also encourage clients to be kind to themselves by being factual when formulating a response and not accept that everything they do must be at "Wonder Woman" level. My point is we generally don't question the self-assessment made by our male counterparts so why do we buy in to an unrealistic expectation for ourselves?

But the other side of the coin is thornier for most women, me included. We are embarrassed at or overly harsh when identifying our challenges. A universal trait among those I coach is the ease with which they berate themselves for being human. It is an interesting balancing act—trying not to be " Wonder Woman" while embracing being human, with our feet firmly planted on the ground, accepting our imperfections.

I urge my clients to be factual, to step away from their internal critic and to ask how they would guide a colleague with a similar challenge. Lastly, I ask them to consider if they are making too much out of very little, meaning to you it is huge but to others it is a non-issue.

I learned to step away from my internal critic and bring the same evaluative ability to myself as I provide to others. This began years ago when I was called out by someone I was coaching. I was assisting her with developing a more mature process to address her challenges. I urged her to be clear and concise in her questions and statements and to avoid her inner critic. She stopped me in my tracks by saying until I demonstrated what I wanted, she was not about to attempt it. As I heard myself say this was not about me, I realized I would readily share my strengths but avoided discussing my weaknesses or challenges. So, I acknowledged her point and told her I would talk about a few of my challenges in our next meeting. In return I would expect her to be prepared to do the same.

My client was spot on. I had always avoided looking at the challenges that held me back. Now I had to face two or three aspects of my behavior that created more problems than necessary. Because this was difficult for me to face, I developed a framework to identify and address areas I needed to work on. I broke it into three categories:

1. Where was I good enough?
2. What would I never be good at in a gazillion years?
3. What did I truly need to rectify to be the leader I wanted to be?

The first two categories eased me into the thinking I needed to do but had for so long avoided. I must confess that I did not accomplish everything in a week, but having a framework brought clarity and gave me a way to stop avoiding my challenges that I still use today.

1. **Where was I good enough?**

The good enough area is comprised of skills and competencies that I need but don't need to be the best at or anywhere near perfect. When I thought about how I interpreted "the best," I realized my overcompetitive nature was creating pseudo-challenges where none should

exist. The near-perfect measure is the fallacy I bought into from childhood – that I had to be superlative in whatever I was doing. Talk about wasting time and energy! Just identifying behaviors that fit into either category gave me room to breathe and shift my focus to what mattered: my challenges.

2. **What would I never be good at in a gazillion years?**

The next category – never in a gazillion years – provided perspective on skills that, in my desire to always improve, I was wasting valuable time and energy on. As I built my list, I realized that I had in fact turned this category into a strength area.

Without consciously realizing it I hired people who were good at things I was not. Once trust was established between us, I gave them direction and latitude to own their areas. This realization was a turning point for me, and I shifted from honing my ability to do things to advancing the intangible skills and behaviors needed to be a successful leader.

The last category was where I needed to focus and spend time really thinking about what I needed to work on to be a better leader. This gave me pause and challenged me in ways I had not imagined.

3. What did I truly need to rectify to be the leader I wanted to be?

What were my greatest challenges at that time? First, I needed to be more patient with others and less egotistical about my ability to process information quickly, to see patterns and to imagine difference. Now the fact that I can do those things is very much a strength, but the fact that I would be impatient with someone who took a bit more time to get to the same place, well that was a huge barrier to my becoming a good leader.

What I came to is that, in my current state, I would not want to work for me. I lacked an understanding of what it meant to respect others. I needed to consistently respect others the way I wanted to be respected. Simple to say but so very complicated to make real. With that at the forefront of my thinking I began to shift from impatience to awareness that there is more than one way to accomplish a task and that being quick did not always translate into being best.

I identified the second area I needed to rectify was how rapidly I would ramp up to the fight portion of the fight-or-flight reaction. I was proudly pugnacious and more than willing to go to war to demonstrate the correctness of my thinking. In other words, if a colleague thought there was something wrong with my idea, I ramped up for the attack. Say that I was off track and I would practically snort in derision. While this was difficult to face, I could readily recall a number of situations I needlessly went to war over.

I knew if I did not address both issues, I would never actually accomplish what I wanted from my career. I began to tackle both issues and surprisingly found myself becoming a better listener and questioner. While neither has been fully laid to rest, I now engage in productive dialogue, not a sparring match. I now understand that a fight is rarely necessary and, oh yes, when I think I am just too smart I turn on *Jeopardy* and find equilibrium!

As you move to the exercises in this chapter and you find you are uncomfortable with what is posed, ask yourself why. Allow the confidence of knowing you are doing good work fill you with pride and use the confidence to address those habits you must change. Often those I coach get stuck in a useless cycle of *mea culpa* rather than acknowledging the challenge and identifying steps to changing the behavior that will result in becoming a better professional and leader.

14

Chapter 2 Workbook

Knowing Yourself as a Professional

Use my three-question framework to move you beyond your challenges. Be honest and direct.

1. Where am I good enough?

2. What will I never be good at in a gazillion years and I'm just fine with that?

3. What do I truly need to rectify to be the leader I want to be?

Here are two tips for recognizing where you need to change and where you have changed:

Tip 1: Once you have identified your challenges and bad habits and begun to make change, make declarative statements that reset your and others' thinking about who you are versus who you were. In a meeting, statements such as "The old Lalia may have said XYZ, but the improved Lalia would like you to consider ABC." I did this because as my colleagues readied themselves for my fight persona, I put forth a different version and called their attention to the leader I had become.

Tip 2: At least twice a year ask yourself four simple questions that require an honest, direct response. Compare your replies over time to gauge your progress. The term honest refers to a balanced critique absent of gender influence that so many women have bought into (men are assertive, women are aggressive). A direct response refers to an absence of sidesteps and vague replies to avoid looking or sounding egotistical.

Four self-assessment questions to be answered honestly and directly.

---

1. What is your most dominant positive trait?

2. What is your most problematic habit? Think of a habit that classifies you. Do you repeatedly say, "I'm sorry"? Do you end your sentences with a question when they should be stated in the declarative?

3. What are two or three professional challenges/ issues/shortcomings you must address?

4. What are the two or three professional strengths you rely upon regularly?

Chapter 3

What we see depends mainly

on what we look for.

–John Lubbock

Knowing the View Others Have of You

Key chapter points

- Effective use of formal assessments to advance your leadership skills and behaviors
- Using a modified Andy Grove decision-making technique
- Tips to consider when reading your reviews and assessments

In the previous chapter, the focus was on developing a realistic self-view of your professional and leadership abilities and behaviors. The flip side is to better understand and use the feedback from others about their view of you as a leader and professional.

Among those I have coached, the great majority of their companies embrace systematic assessments (i.e., 360- degree feedback, peer reviews) to provide a comprehensive view of colleagues,' bosses' and employees' perception of leaders. Much time, money and effort are put into identifying and embedding assessments into the formal activities and responsibilities of the business. Systematically, assessments are conducted, analyzed and reviewed, then checked off the list of must- dos until the next time around. But even the companies that schedule meetings to review the results do so in an elementary manner and often fail to draw meaningful connections that assist leaders in advancing their skills and behaviors.

As a coach I ask for copies of the client's most recent assessments. My first question after reading the evaluations is, "What changes did you make in response to the conclusions and recommendations?" More often than not little has been addressed. Two camps dominate: those who ignore or argue about the results and those who over-internalize the information and blame themselves for not being a better leader.

Much of what I do as an executive coach is help clients shift their perspective. Rather than being angry or self-condemning, I suggest taking one question at a time and moving from the subjective (personal) to the objective (factual) view. Sounds easy, huh? Consider adopting the method used by Andy Grove, founder of Intel, who when faced with making a controversial or risky decision would ask himself "If I were replaced tomorrow, what would my successor do?" This approach enabled him to remove the angst and made room for an open-minded, dispassionate review of the facts. I modify this question and ask, "If the assessment were about a trusted colleague what advice would you have for them on each of the points made?" By shifting perspective one can expand how you see and receive reviews.

"If I were replaced tomorrow, what would my successor do?"

Tips for reading your assessments:

- Read each separately and systematically think about

what is being said about you as a professional and a leader. A defined approach should serve as a road map for improving and updating how others view you. When you begin to move toward anger or angst use the modified Andy Grove question: What advice would you have for a trusted colleague? Work to gain perspective. Do you agree with what is said? Why or why not? Is there old information that needs updating?

- Avoid homing in on the comments that are negative or hurtful. Do not allow your feelings to overtake your rational thinking.

- Do you readily accept what others think of you as a colleague or leader rather than weighing it against your own solid understanding of who you are? As you read the comments, know why you agree, question or disagree with a comment. Think about your reaction and maintain an equilibrium of purpose.

- Reflect on how often you question your self-measure of a job well done and if you give more credit to someone else's opinion about your performance.

Chapter 3 Workbook

Knowing the View Others Have of You

Take each of your assessments and individually review them to answer the following questions:

- Identify specific statements and concerns peers or direct reports have about you. From your perspective is the statement substantive or hearsay? Why? Is the concern out of date but continues to be passed on? Why?

- Specifically examine what your boss has to say about you. Is the characterization based on past events or issues? If so, how have you changed?

- Identify specific statements where others indicate you excel. Do you agree? Why? What must you do to maintain the level of excellence?

- After reviewing each of your assessments, pull the information you gained into a summary that highlights consistent themes, such as repeated phrases or concepts that shine a positive or negative light on your leadership and professional abilities and skills. Turn the information into a narrative that demonstrates who you are versus who you were.

- Practice using the modified Andy Grove question when you get stuck "What advice would I give a trusted colleague if this were their assessment?"

Chapter 4

Don't judge a book by its cover.

- Mr. Tulliver in *The Mill on the Floss*

–George Eliot

Owning Your First Impression

Key chapter points
- Why owning your first impression matters
- Redefining the cover to your book
- Identifying your own rush to judgment about others

A necessary but often overlooked aspect to the work you have done in chapters 2 and 3 is adjusting inaccurate first impressions. This has become one of the more intriguing coaching challenges I have encountered as high-powered, wicked smart, accomplished individuals do not own the first impressions they make when moving to a new organization or new area.

Owning the impression means knowing whether or not it is on target, but many either do not care (hubris) or are unaware (naïveté). By and far, all are enormously talented in the hard skills but often dismiss the impact of their underdeveloped social skills if they make a negative first impression.

When I take on a new client I begin the coaching process with a series of interviews of direct reports, peers and boss. During the course of the interviews, I ask about first and subsequent impressions for the purpose of developing a comprehensive picture of others' view of my client's strengths and abilities. The impression questions are asked of all I interview to identify commonly held themes and to avoid embracing one person's perspective or bias. The following is an amalgamation of feedback I received during interviews highlighting the difficulties that can occur when first impressions are not corrected or dealt with.

A story:

Often the detail provided by peers about their first meeting with the new executive was universally detrimental. The damaging impression solidified and was passed on to new hires as part of their on-boarding even if they did not report to the new executive.

In my interviews I would be told the new executive was the real deal as her abilities and skills were plentiful. Clients were described as visionary, innovative and knowledgeable. But the lasting or dominant impression held of the new executive was negative using terms such as abrasive, impatient, short-tempered and demanding. Overlooked was the client's self-confidence, ability to get to the root of the problem, and willingness to challenge the status quo.

And therein lies the problem — confidence was interpreted as hubris. Questioning a statement was seen and heard as threatening. Clients were seen as unlikeable and other abilities such as quickly getting to an issue were not valued. The first impression formed was of an executive with a confidence and directness expected in men but problematic for new women executives. Peers tagged my clients as difficult and egotistical know-it-alls. The instantaneous judging that occurred impeded their success.

Most of the women I have coached are frustrated with the one-dimensional interpretation of them as aggressive, know-it-all, sharp tongued, abrupt or unwilling to listen. And the interpretation is often accompanied by a belief that the promotion was linked to other descriptors that refer to the color of one's skin, sexuality or ethnicity. As the initial negative impression solidifies and is passed throughout the organization and to new employees, it does not matter if it is correct. What matters is the collective agreement that the woman was a token and had not earned her leadership position. The damage of not revisiting a skewed first impression can negatively impact peer and direct report relationships and cause decisions to consistently be put under a high-powered microscope. Ignoring preconceived and set notions is problematic as it allows a false narrative to spread throughout the organization. Owning the cover of the book on you is a vital activity in advancing your career.

It is not enough to understand that first impressions carry imprecise judgments; it is what you do to reframe the classic micro-decisions of judging a book by its cover that matters. I suggest my clients do "spot checks." Periodically ask a colleague, direct report or boss their view of your behavior or approach. The key is to listen and engage in a discussion that allows for better understanding by both sides. Be proactive about the perspective others have of your ability or behavior. Such a conversation can be done in the moment if you are prepared to do so. But be aware that a one-on-one exchange at a later date could be more beneficial.

Know your end goal is to shift perceptions, not to be right or to prove another wrong. Whether you directly hear a false impression or learn secondhand, maintain your emotional equilibrium, ask questions and be willing to listen to the response even when it sounds biased. What you actually say in response depends on context, but what is clear is those who do not let their emotions rule are far more effective in reframing how others view their leadership ability.

In my experience, there is a persistent difference in how men and women are judged as leaders. The first impression of men newly hired or promoted can be seen as abrasive, short-tempered, overly demanding, and overly self-assured but their peers and direct reports were able to overlook their failings and focus on their positive attributes, generally their knowledge and expertise. However, when women exhibited similar negative qualities, their peers and others tended to overlook the positives instead focusing their attention on qualities viewed as unbecoming in a woman leader.

An unexpected benefit to owning the cover on the book of you is a greater awareness of your own biases, assumptions and judgments you readily make about others. Recognizing how you are being framed should open up your eyes and ears to your own preconceived notions about your team, colleagues and bosses. Your one-dimensional view of others limits the success of the business, your coworkers and yourself. Acknowledging that you judge a book by its cover can be a most freeing and at the same time a discomforting exploration.

Chapter 4 Workbook

Owning Your First Impression

Over the next two weeks spend time considering how people view you. This could mean identifying an inaccurate first impression that became a repeated story told over and over until it gained best seller status shared by others with conviction and belief.

1. Consider the first impression you make. Does your perception match the impression formed by your peers, team and boss?

2. What steps will you take to address any inaccurate perceptions? Spot checks? Correcting misconceptions? Asking questions when hearing a false narrative?

3. Consider how you judge others and quickly and incorrectly create a false cover of them. What will you change to lessen your own biases when forming impressions of others?

Chapter 5

Be yourself,

everyone else is already taken.

−Oscar Wilde

Embrace Who You Are

Key chapter points
- Not fitting in is not a negative aspect of your career
- Embrace how you don't fit in and view it as the secret ingredient that defines your uniqueness
- Identify others who never fit in but succeed

In fourth-grade civics class, I learned anyone could be president, which was wonderful to hear. Not that I understood, but from that I took to heart that I could be anything, anything at all. I could be president of the United States of America! In class I learned all men are created equal and, in my naïveté, I thought that meant all people, any people. It was far later in my development I learned it only meant a select portion of society and so I began to realize I didn't fit in.

Soon after, at a birthday party for a relative, I told all there I wanted to be president of the country. The adults laughed and a male relative said, "Oh Lalia, only men are presidents." Well that only strengthened my desire to be something, but what I didn't know. I only knew I didn't want to be what my mom urged me to consider – be a teacher with a pension or a nun! Those jobs seemed to be confining, safe and just too not me.

The Oscar Wilde quote has great meaning for me that I need to be myself as I was not going to "fit in," be the "good girl," be "seen and seldom heard." I didn't understand why I should try to fit in. Sometime around the age of 14, I began a journey to learn about women who didn't fit in because I knew I was never going to.

Women who didn't fit in but claimed themselves and succeeded in spite of what society said became my role models. Women like Brownie Wise who developed the Tupperware party and established sales methods that we still use today. Women like my neighbor lady Angie, an associate professor of business at the University of Wisconsin-Madison, who lived with her sister, a medical doctor. Both were college graduates at a time when most women did not earn a degree much less work full-time outside the home.

I embraced this early lesson and approach throughout my professional career and urged my clients to recognize if they faced similar challenges of not fitting in. Their focus or perspective should not be on how to fit in. Instead, I encouraged them to embrace how they don't fit in, to view it as their secret ingredient that defines their uniqueness. Rather than viewing not fitting in as a determent, revel in taking the unconventional path and view conformity as uninspiring.

View conformity as uninspiring.

Consider if you waste emotional energy trying to fit your square peg into a round hole. But coming to grips with your difference is a challenge and for many it is a reach too far. So, I suggest an approach I call "how to slowly embrace not fitting in." Just like a pair of shoes that are too small and pinch your toes, embracing who you are can seem painful and ill-fitting as often women are accultured to fulfill pre-determined societal roles. Even the term *leader* is deeply embedded in our thoughts as male and so you may find yourself having to consistently redefine your style to new team members because you do not fit their archetype.

I suggest you identify where or how you don't fit in. Look at whether it positively or negatively matters to your success. If positive, that is your secret ingredient! If negative, figure out how to put it away. Notice I didn't say figure out why you view it negatively. Not everything you learn or know about yourself has to be explored; more important is making the change. Too many use the why exploration as a way to avoid change and not take responsibility.

The work in this chapter can be hard in that you must acknowledge where you don't fit the leader stereotype. Here are a few of my differences: I weigh more than what is the expected size of a successful person. My hair is gray/white. I have lines that lead others to see me as past my prime. I present myself as an equal regardless of who is in the room and my confidence can be viewed as negative – aggressive, confrontational. So, what does that mean? It means for me I have to be comfortable with who I am. I remember that I can impact first impressions by the way I accept myself without letting another's judgment alter my confidence in my professional skills and abilities. I believe it is best to be who I am because "everybody else is taken!"

Chapter 5 Workbook

Embrace Who You Are

Manage how you don't fit in by identifying what you did earlier in your career.

1. What did you do as a less experienced professional when in situations where you didn't fit in you?

2. How did worrying about not fitting in create problems for you?

3. If the same things were to happen today, what would you do differently?

Identify what you have become where you don't fit in:

_____

1. Identify a few aspects of the leadership stereotype where you don't fit in. Describe what this means for you.

2. What positive differences do you have from your colleagues and from other leaders?

3. Which of these differences is your secret ingredient?

4. How do you celebrate not fitting in while succeeding?

5. Have you explained your approach of not fitting in to those you mentor?

Chapter 6

It's not only moving that creates new starting points. Sometimes all it takes is a subtle shift in perspective, an opening of the mind, an intentional pause and reset, or a new route to start to see new options and new possibilities.

–Kristin Armstrong

Perspective Matters

Key chapter points
- Understanding the benefits of shifting your perspective
- Realizing that listening is a skill
- Regulating your emotional responses matters

How often on your daily commute to work have you found yourself at a stop light wondering how you got there? The action or event becomes so ordinary, so repetitive that we zone out and no longer see or hear what's going on. We go on automatic pilot and let our muscle memory take over so we look beyond what is right in front of us. We do this at work when we encounter repeat problems or an employee that *always* complains or when we bring a set of expectations to a situation before listening to the briefing.

In the course of coaching scores of clients and reflecting on my own experience, it is clear to me that for all but a few the ability to objectively see and hear others is a challenging skill. It requires patience, consideration, attentiveness and a willingness to think logically.

The very measure of self-regulation is demonstrated by:
1. Your willingness to control the desire to assume you know what the person is going to say or want.

2. Changing from being a fixer to a coach to help your team to learn to think and solve problems.
3. Focusing on what is being said rather than stop listening so you can frame the perfect retort.
4. Lessening the dramatic leap that creates mountains out of molehills.

Picasso's *The Bull* is a lithograph series of 11 drawings created in late 1945 depicting the animal from the actual to the abstract. Each drawing is a slightly different perspective and an image of a bull beginning with a fully drawn realistic animal and ending in an impressionistic view drawn in a few strokes of the pencil. The grouping for me is a wonderful representation of shifting perspective. I use the series to demonstrate the subjective nature of perspective and as a tool for helping clients learn how to shift their business and leadership perspective.

When I show the drawings there are two common reactions. For some the more abstract drawings are without value for only the actual bull drawing has meaning for them, while others are pulled in by the symbolism and repelled by the fixed form. Someone who steps back to see the entire series and then focuses on the differences in a sequential fashion is the more unusual response.

I encourage everyone I coach to shift their perspective when faced with repetitive issues, to find a different frame of reference to avoid making assumptions, and to try a different approach rather than leap to a conclusion. We all fall prey to making mountains out of molehills, meaning we take a trivial matter and elevate it to a momentous challenge that requires our full attention and resources. It plays out in the workplace as someone who overreacts, easily becoming a drama queen when confronted with a minor obstacle. One very common example of such behavior is over worrying about a mistake you made. It dominates your thinking and freezes your recovery as it takes on a life of its own. Perhaps you even go so far as to decide the mistake could ruin your career.

I readily make assumptions when it would be far better to stop and think. Because this is such a challenge for me, I researched the concept to help me in my quest to temper how quickly I made assumptions at work. I broke it up into three categories:

The good: Those assumptions that are shortcuts to make us more efficient and productive so no need to address these.

The bad: Meaning I assume something is true or false without any proof, or I want to believe something will happen without any facts to support it when clearly these should be identified and dealt with.

The ugly: When my assumptions trump logic and reason and I don't want to change my thinking because I am comfortable making assumptions.

To grapple with the ugly assumptions, you must be willing to face yourself and do something about it. Instead of jumping to a conclusion, take a breath, relax and ask a question that will assist you in understanding more completely what is needed to address the situation or issue. Increase your ability to get to the root of the problem rather than assuming you know what your colleague is going to say. Stop focusing on your experience and focus on them, asking better questions and staying in the moment rather than thinking about what you will say. Take

Take a breath, relax and ask a question

yourself in hand when you feel or hear yourself take things out of proportion. Step back and do something to break your impulse to overreact. Breathe. Ask a question. Break the tension within yourself.

Shifting your perspective allows you to hear and see more than one possibility or solution. It comes from thinking differently about your job as a leader. I often say to my clients you are not to be the one with all the answers. A main responsibility is to grow those who report to you and that means developing their ability to think and to develop solutions.

I learned about shifting perspective in a difficult and amazing manner as a relatively inexperienced consultant.

A story:

Some 30 years ago I was given an assignment through a contract my boss had with the United Nations Development Programme (UNDP) to conduct a three-week workshop in Karachi, Pakistan, on expanding international tourism to Southeast Asia. I had never traveled outside the contiguous United States at that

44

point and didn't have a passport. I went on what turned out to be one of the seminal experiences of my life.

The trip was a series of firsts for me: my first-time flying business and first class, my first experience in a non-Western country and culture, and my first time being the only American in the room. Imagine me arriving in Karachi at 2:30 a.m. after 20-some hours flying, coming down the steps to the tarmac, it was late November, and I was dressed for winter not for humidity and high temperatures of southern Pakistan. I did not do my homework. I assumed about the weather and was I wrong. I ended up wearing three outfits repeatedly since my winter wardrobe wasn't appropriate.

As we went through the airport and customs I was taken by how quiet and orderly it was as my experience at U.S. airports had people eagerly awaiting inside for arrivals. I leapt to the conclusion it was so late that everyone was home in bed. This misconception struck me full on as I walked out of the airport into a sea of hundreds, if not thousands, of people, lots of noise and bright lights, colors and smells. People were calling for my attention in a language I did not understand. It was overwhelming and breathtaking, amazing and a bit frightening.

Two days later I met one woman and 12 men, tourism professionals from Nepal, Sri Lanka, Pakistan, India, Bangladesh and Myanmar, who had come to participate in the workshop. I was there to share my technical knowledge but, in the end, I learned far more about myself and cultural similarities and differences.

One experience stands out and demonstrates why gaining perspective rather than making assumptions matters. I had brought sunflower seeds in the shell with me for a snack and during a break on the third day of the workshop I took a handful out to munch on. The first question asked of me when we returned was what had I been eating during the break. I did not expect the question. More importantly, I was astounded by my failure to think differently and realized I needed to not only talk about the snack but the much larger picture of the differences that would be encountered by travelers when visiting areas outside their daily routine.

No one in the group had ever seen much less eaten a sunflower seed so I explained you could eat it in the shell or crack the shell with your teeth and only eat the seed. This led to a discussion of what they ate for a quick and easy snack and how they would market and explain the experience to an international traveler. I remember so vividly thinking how I had not given a thought to what they or I took for granted and saw as universal or needing no explanation. I realized how shortsighted I was, how my perception was skewed. From that moment on I took a different approach to my workshops and leading others. But the key was from then on, I asked more questions to ensure what I assumed was in fact reality.

Note: It is amazing how much the world has changed over the past three decades. We know so much more about new and unexperienced destinations before we go as the information is at our fingertips. As well, we are more knowledgeable about cultural and societal differences.

My experience in Pakistan made me realize that to advance my thinking, teaching, coaching and interactions I must shift and learn to listen and think differently, to stop jumping to conclusions, making assumptions and to not making mountains out of molehills. To shift my perspective, I paid attention to what I was doing and saw very clearly what a poor listener I was. I was too busy figuring out my response and so I would miss what the person was actually saying. In my desire to demonstrate I was a manager, I made assumptions about people or situations rather than ask questions to make certain I understood. Rather than get the facts straight I would jump to a conclusion and make ill-informed decisions.

I made some rules for myself to limit the negative and immature behaviors. To this day I struggle mightily with controlling my knee-jerk reactions and making assumptions when I should not. This is my way of saying while my rules might be useful, they only work if you practice them!

1. Limit the number of assumptions you make each day. Instead, ask for more information so you learn the value of not leaping to a conclusion before you more fully understand the circumstances.

2. Organize your thinking before meetings to prepare yourself to listen and ask questions.

3. Know your hot buttons so when you hear something that triggers an emotional reaction you don't move to make a mountain out of a molehill. When you feel yourself ramping up, take a deep breath and sit back. Rather than make statements, ask questions or take a moment and listen.

4. Listen with an open mind. Ask for clarification when you would rather assume.

If you do leap to a conclusion and become aware of it, stop, take a breath and back up. No need for *mea culpa*, just "Let me back up and ask a question."

Chapter 6 Workbook

Perspective Matters

1. Identify when you are more likely to make an assumption, leap to a conclusion or make a mountain out of a molehill. Take each phrase separately.

For each situation identify why you stopped listening. This is not to be a laundry list, but do you find that in certain situations or with a certain type of individual you quit listening to formulate your reply, or you stop listening and interrupt because you know what they are going to say?

2. Recall a time when you overreacted to a colleague's remark. Using your new perspective, how would you react now?

3. How can you rewind the tape when you've jumped to a conclusion?

Chapter 7

The greater danger for most of us lies not in setting our aim too high and falling short; but in setting our aim too low and achieving our mark.

–Michelangelo

Choose to Be

Key chapter points

- Combating the contagion of mediocrity
- Recognizing you have a choice to rise above
- Understanding your definition of mediocrity

The quote by Michelangelo speaks to my very core. As one of the greatest painters, sculptors, poets and thinkers in history, I often turn to him for inspiration and joy. When I stumbled across this quote, it was as if he was speaking directly to me. I have always struggled with individuals and organizations that accept so-so results and low standards. I believe that mediocrity is contagious. We rise or fall to the level of expectation that is set for us by ourselves first and then others. If I tell myself "I can," I am far more likely to accomplish something than when I tell myself "maybe."

Any job has tedious elements that matter but can drag you into mediocrity. This is one of the greatest *hidden* professional challenges. The battle against mediocrity, of cutting corners, of knowing you could do better but instead you stop caring or become bored or decide not to bother trying. In other words, the passion you had upon taking the job dissipates and frustration or dissatisfaction sets in.

When this happens, dare yourself to let go of what has been and work toward what can be. Rather than focusing on problems look for solutions. Ask better questions, engage in risk and innovation that questions the status quo and establishes expectations for thinking differently. See what really is, not what we have been programmed to see or want to see. Think outside the norm and believe it is OK not to accept something at face value and instead listen intently and consider a different approach. Rather than dismiss an idea or concept because it is different or difficult, be brave enough to consider it. I offer a story as it reflects much of what I am suggesting to you.

Think outside the norm and believe it is OK.

A story:

I worked in the hospitality industry beginning in high school as a dishwasher and bus girl (versus bus boy) in a busy supper club in my hometown. In my senior year in high school, I was promoted to waitress. I watched those I worked with to understand what made one or two waitresses so good and the rest OK. I learned the tangible skills (knowing the menu, balancing a full tray, having multiple pens available), which took some time. But what I saw in the really good waitresses was that to be successful waiting tables some elements had to flow naturally. Your smile had to be genuine. You needed to be interested in your customers. You had to be prepared to make suggestions. You had to be fast and organized. You needed a good memory, and an eye for detail. There was so much more to the job than one might expect and because I wanted to be among the very best, I decided to compete with myself. How many tables could I handle? How many orders could I memorize without writing them down? How fast could I get to each table once they had sat down?

This challenge gave me a goal to accomplish for each shift. I made it about more than my tips and unconsciously moved my focus off the tedious aspects of serving (getting asked the same questions over and over) and consistently raised my expectations for myself. (Was it a mistake-free shift? Did I connect with my customers?) I became one of the best waitresses because each and every shift I expected myself to be better.

Be that individual who decides not to be mediocre, who decides to be her best as that person can transform, inspire loyalty and generate a clear and consistent strategy. It doesn't matter how inconsequential a task seems, realize that it all matters. Act maturely, demonstrating you understand your role and that of your colleagues. Be someone willing to take a risk and when you don't succeed, take the lesson learned and analyze another way forward that is smarter and better developed. It is a daunting and exhilarating role that is not for everyone. But oh, when you meet, work with, and learn from an individual who is not mediocre you will advance your own ability and move from any whiff of mediocrity. I believe there are extraordinary professionals who demand more of themselves and all who work with them. It is just harder to find them in this age of hype and artifice. Follow Michelangelo and set a standard to never be mediocre, to consistently challenge myself to be better.

Chapter 7 Workbook

Choose to Be

Managing the battle against mediocrity

1. As a professional, how do you define mediocrity?

2. How do you explain your definition to your team, colleagues and boss?

3. Think of a time in your work life that you rose above, fought against mediocrity and drove yourself to greater success.

4. Currently what drives you through the best and the worst, what sustains you through mediocrity?

5. Are there situations when you stop caring or stop trying in your current job?

6. What happens when you choose not to be your best?

Chapter 8

Winning is great, sure, but if you are really going to do something in life, the secret is learning how to lose. Nobody goes undefeated all the time. If you can pick up after a crushing defeat, and go on to win again, you are going to be a champion someday.

−Wilma Rudolph

Mistakes are a fact of life.
It is the response to the error that counts.
−Nikki Giovanni

Moving Beyond the Fear of Failure

Key chapter points

- Failure is not the issue – it is what we do on the rebound that matters
- Think before acting, not after
- Preparation matters

I found two quotes that speak to me about embracing failure and rather than select one over the other, I went with both. There is no rule about one quote per chapter – that was a self-imposed dictum – and if any chapter should encourage difference, this is the one. Both statements point to an undeniable truth – you will fail. But it is not in the fail that one actually loses; that is measured by what one does on the rebound and how we learn from and grow from the experience. Risk, innovation and change often result in failure and the most common culprit is insufficient thinking. I position failure as an opportunity to learn and succeed the next time. I do not fear failing but actually relish the post-mortem and I'm especially keen to understand "how to" or "how not to."

One of my favorite failure stories occurred shortly after I had earned my doctoral degree at George Washington University.

A story:

I went to the dean of the school where I served as a program director and instructor to ask for a raise. I thought my request was reasonable and timely but within 15 seconds after asking I was told "no" in definitive terms. Wasn't going to happen, not what I had asked for, not $5, nothing, nada, nope. I couldn't believe it. My case was ironclad from my perspective. I had taken on an additional assignment, gotten my doctorate and taught a full load of classes. What more did he want from me? Well, the short answer was to leave his office. (No joke intended that is how my question was answered.) What more could I have done? How could he treat me that way? Everyone knows you get a raise after you achieve a higher degree! I was wronged! I left his office and actually vowed to get another position at another university. And that is what I did when six months later I became a dean at a small university in Connecticut with a far better salary as a tenured professor. I never looked back, but I do take satisfaction in turning lemons into champagne. (Who cares if you can get lemonade?!)

My failure goes directly to the addiction we have to act and to fire before we even aim. I learned from my ill-fated request for a higher salary that no matter how much I believed I was right, I needed to prepare a rock-solid argument. I needed to prepare for various scenarios, and I needed to understand the art of negotiation. From the failure to secure a raise, I learned the value of thinking before acting, the art of turning a no into a maybe, and how to use failure to propel myself to unexpected places.

People who say "I never fail" or "I am afraid to fail" are likely to achieve the low mark Michelangelo described in the quote found in the previous chapter. Fear of failure is an attitude that can destroy the possibility of success. Such fear can be all-consuming akin to a blackhole in space that draws everything into its wake, never to be seen again. Fear of failing diminishes one's spirit, dampening the sense of possibility in exchange for marginality. Allowing fear to dominate your ability to take a risk and to dampen innovation destroys your ability to embrace the challenges you face.

Another way to view fear of failure is as a life not well-lived. The overly cautious will never transform or create. Those who seek the pseudo-comfort of conformity will never inspire change. One need not jump without looking, but not jumping is the issue.

Chapter 8 Workbook

Moving Beyond the Fear of Failure

1. Identify a scenario in which you failed. What did you learn from the situation and how did you grow from the experience?

2. What is it about failure that is your greatest stumbling block?

3. How can you learn to think before you act?

4. If you can believe that failure is necessary to eventual success, what will you do to move beyond your current comfort zone?

Chapter 9

Our chief want is someone
who will inspire us to be what we know we
could be.

−Ralph Waldo Emerson

Inspire Yourself and Others

Key chapter points

- Know what inspires you to be more
- Understand how to use negative inspiration
- Use inspiration to reach beyond yourself

It was another experience with Michelangelo that defined what reaching beyond myself meant. When I first saw Michelangelo's statue, *David* in Florence, Italy, my mind exploded. The sculpture is nothing short of miraculous. It is so exquisite I could do nothing at first but allow myself to be filled with wonder, to be in awe of the skill, determination and vision that could take a block of marble and create what is as close to divine as I will see in my lifetime.

Looking at *David*, I was filled with a sense that nothing is impossible. From that experience I began to understand the benefits of inspiration. That does not mean I won't be challenged or that I will suddenly find the answer. No, for me, it means that I am no longer holding myself back, I am not letting my fear drive me and I am confident in my abilities. I realized inspiration comes at unexpected moments and while I can never create a statue, I can use the inspiration I experienced when I saw Michelangelo's work. I could keep the feeling and understanding within me to be more, to be better and therefore to create *my* own *David*. I chose to inspire others and to move them forward to accomplishment. I am proud that in my

66

career I have been able to bring people with me as I succeeded and, regardless of the impact, I consistently helped them transition to positions of greater responsibility and joy. I chose to succeed in achieving short- and long-term goals. Rather than setting resolutions (I will get the monthly report in on time), I began to set goals with measurable expectations (the monthly report will be submitted within three business days following the end of month and will include X, Y and Z) which allowed me to focus more effectively and more efficiently use my time. I chose to take an idea, create the vision and accomplish it. As an example, I started a consulting business as an extension of my career in higher education and built it into a successful enterprise that established me as a thought leader in the areas of leadership development and strategy.

During a coaching engagement I assisted an executive in turning a situation that was potentially a career ender and instead to use it as "negative" inspiration. Think about that for a minute. You can shift your perspective on something negative and use it to propel you to greater success. This client had to present to her company's board of directors once a month. Certain members of the board were not supportive of her being in her position and at each board meeting attempted to chip away at her boss's confidence in her performance. It became a battle royal as their goal became clear: They, not she, would be the last men standing. She decided leaving was not a choice and when she brought it to our session, she knew her challenge was beyond her previous experience.

As we worked through the attempt to discredit, diminish and destroy her work and her reputation, I advised her to use the situation to inspire her. At first, she was unable to imagine how anything so insidious could be inspiring. I urged her to shift her perspective, to stop giving them control and to consider an approach that could turn the focus from her to them. This meant she had to set aside the emotion of the situation and consider what she knew about the individuals. When did they go on the attack? Was there a pattern to the attacks? How did others on the board react? Using the questions as a guide for moving forward, she began to control the narrative and working with the CEO was able to establish different rules of conduct for board meetings. For example, she went to the chair of the board and asked him to assist her by offering a positive take on her performance for the CEO and the board.

I learned the value of negative inspiration the hard way. The story of meeting my new boss who managed from a negative space provides a valuable example of the insidious aspects of power, which inspired me to consciously decide to never be like him, taking inspiration from an unusual situation.

A story:

A memory that remains as vivid as the day it occurred was my first meeting with my new boss. I walked into his office, he extended his hand, and as I took it, he pulled me to him and very quietly said, "I want you to fear me." As I tried to step back and look at him, the absurdity of the statement hit me, and I laughed as I attempted to process the situation. In a micro-second I thought he was either deranged or an extremely weird person at best. But in the next micro-second I realized he was serious. He would not let me step away when I made an initial attempt, exerting a dominant hold to demonstrate control both physically and emotionally.

My reaction was immediate: "You will have my resignation this afternoon as I will not work for someone who asks me to fear them." The words sprang out of my mouth without any thought! He stepped back, let go of my hand and asked me to sit down so we could talk about what I had just said. I could see he was taken aback by my immediate declaration rejecting him. Suffice it to say he capitulated his position and offered me a sizeable raise to stay with one caveat – I could not tell others of our agreement that I did not have to fear him.

Setting aside the unusual nature of this set of circumstances, I used the negative experience to inspire and define what I would never be as a leader. I was not in the position to leave my job for many reasons, but I was also not going to remain shaken to my core. I mean, who says something like that? It took me about five days to process his remarks, my reaction and the fact I had to continue working with him at least for the short term. I put it into perspective and used it to gain clarity. From that day to now I committed to act differently when in a position of authority knowing and keeping a set of ethical standards. Prior to this experience I had not clearly defined my own ethics and values as a leader. That boss taught me valuable lessons of what not to be that I use as a touchstone to this very day.

Note: My experience occurred some two decades ago and the type of negative leadership, while never right, was more accepted. The client example took place more recently, but it does demonstrate that intimidation as a norm continues unabated in the workplace. The response by my client was more direct than mine as she asked for and received support from the CEO and board chair to end the questionable behavior of board members. While there are still issues with one board member, she has shifted her perspective and chooses when and how she will react rather than allowing the negative behavior to determine her reaction.

Chapter 9 Workbook

Inspire Yourself and Others

To inspire what we know we can be:

1. Determine what inspires you, whether it is a work of art, a speech, an event or the example of a life wonderfully lived that allows you to move beyond yourself.

2. How does the inspiration push you to break through whatever barriers are stopping you from becoming the leader who is able to positively influence a team?

3. How does your inspiration provide a lift, give you a greater sense of purpose and direction, or serve as a catalyst for advancement of individuals and goals?

4. What inflames your soul to rise and achieve no matter the challenge you are facing?

5. Have you used a negative experience to inspire you? How?

Chapter 10

I'm a very private person, and when I leave the stage, I leave the stage.

−Helen Reddy

The Public You Versus the Private You

Key chapter points

- Knowing the difference between a public and a private persona
- Using compartmentalization to separate business from personal
- Developing a transition between work you and home you

One of my fondest memories of my mother is lying on her bed watching her dress, do her hair and makeup to get ready to work at the bar and grill she owned with my dad. She had a process for getting ready that she followed start to finish, ending with her choice of earrings. As a young girl I was taken by how wonderful she looked – like a movie star! Thinking about the experience today I still marvel how she was able to go from casual to chic. When she started dressing, she was my mom and then she became Marg, a woman who ran a business.

Many years later in my first job in higher education as an instructor, I recalled my mom's process transforming from housewife (private) to businessperson (public) and decided I should follow a similar process to separate the parts of me best called upon in private moments from those I would rely upon to be the professional I wanted to become. The steps my mom took were enough for her but not for me as my professional maturity was not fully formed. The long and short of it was I needed to grow up and realize that my shortcomings would hinder my advancement. The reality was I knew how to be a college student but the idea that I had to be the adult in the classroom – that my job was to help students learn and grow – this was completely foreign to me. Without realizing it at the time, it was my first step in understanding emotional intelligence and the concept of positive compartmentalization.

Over time I realized I was able to separate or compartmentalize behaviors that belonged with family and friends and to identify characteristics that would not be useful to advancing my career. I don't worry about why I can do it; I just appreciate the fact I can. It was useful as I transitioned from managing areas of a hotel to being a member of the faculty. One particular experience early on in my teaching career defined the difference between public and private and the need to compartmentalize:

A story:

A few weeks into my first semester teaching I was overwhelmed by the amount of work and effort it took to teach four courses, one of which was hotel law. Everything about it was daunting – the subject (dry and complex and I had very little knowledge), the size of the class (120 juniors and seniors), and the time (three hours on Wednesday night). I let my competitive behavior drive me.

This wasn't going to get the best of me, I could be a legal expert! Rather than accept the fact this was not about me showing them, I dug in and gave my best imitation of an egotistical law student. I created an adversarial relationship with the class and the subject and wanted them to see I was far more miserable than they could ever be.

I dreaded midweek, finding ways to avoid the fact I was doing badly. I would up the ante and try to regurgitate as much information as possible, taking on topics I barely understood. Oh, it was bad. What finally pushed me to realize I was the issue occurred on a warm evening in late autumn. Class had just begun, and a guy walks in, calls out a name, starts up the stairs to give one of my students a pizza and a six-pack of beer. I was shocked, and my first instinct was to accept defeat and quit. I was humiliated (all about me). They were laughing at me (I would if the situation were reversed). I was a failure.

And that is when something shifted in one of those situations when everything slows down. It really was pretty funny and something I would have done as a student if in the same situation. I went from wanting to run to realizing this was my "now or never" moment. I knew I could change but first I had to reclaim my position as the instructor and to accept that change was necessary, but that would have to wait as I had to shift the unfolding dynamic. I called out, "Bring that down to the front, NOW." Even though my delivery was somewhat shaky, the guy turned around and gave me the food and drink. The student who had set up the prank began to protest while I opened the pizza box and popped open each beer can. I remember looking at him, thinking what a jerk, which of course made me feel better, but what came out of my mouth was, "If you think you can order just for yourself and not the whole class well then only the flies will eat and drink!" Some students laughed, others smiled, and I relaxed.

The next day I went to an experienced faculty and asked for advice. It crystallized for me when he said, "It's your job to work with students, not be the best student, so work to your strengths, what you know." No more faking it, no more feeling sorry for myself. I had to be prepared to lecture, which really means explaining information in a practical and illustrative fashion, so students were motivated to continue listening and learning.

There it was. I needed to control my impulsive emotional reactions, stop putting myself at the center (that was for the students) and corral my ego. (I wasn't a lawyer and that was OK.) By the end of the semester, I was no longer dreading Wednesdays and I actually began to learn to be a teacher.

I review this situation whenever I struggle as a professional to recall what it takes to be an adult at work. First and foremost, I remind myself not to take others' actions or words personally. I remember to breathe deeply to break my fight response. (I was always ready for the fight, willing to give as good as I got, quick to let my anger rule me.) Instead, I go back to a simple but effective technique: Ask a follow-up question rather than reacting. Take a minute to formulate my response instead of issuing a stinging retaliation. And remember "this is business, don't take it personally." Each of these actions forms the foundation of what is now the workplace Lalia. All this relates to emotional maturity and compartmentalizing behaviors appropriate to personal versus work life.

> *Remember "this is business, don't take it personally."*

In coaching others to grapple with underdeveloped elements of their emotional maturity I share my learned beliefs:

1. We all can avoid taking in statements that could harm our well-being.
2. We can identify behaviors that are not useful to our careers and success.
3. It is so much easier not to take responsibility for actions that are inappropriate.
4. Learning to positively compartmentalize allows you to use the right strengths at the right time.
5. Maturity is not related to one's chronological age and becoming responsible is not a linear or universal experience.

I share what I did to create a public persona that blends everyday strengths with business-appropriate behaviors. To be clear, my example is not the story; the process is the story. My process was to conduct an honest review of my behaviors, read articles that would advance my understanding of how to change a behavior, practice whatever I learned (and practice and practice), look for role models that I wanted to emulate or never be, and realize changing one's behaviors would be an incremental life journey not a quick jaunt.

I identified areas for improvement, a blend of tangible and intangible actions and practices that would move me forward on my journey. Among the tangible changes I made were to be more direct when speaking, which meant I had to bring greater clarity and precision to the words I chose. I lowered the tone of my voice and varied my cadence so not to finish my sentences on a higher timbre, which turns a declarative sentence into a question. I remembered lessons from my childhood about appearance which I turned into my armor – my shoes were always polished, nails and hair shiny and clean, clothes pressed and appropriate to the setting. When I stepped into my high heels, I carried myself with assurance and calm and I left my apprehensions for another time and place. To cement the compartmentalization, I consciously shifted gears when I put my high heels on and took them off.My intangible actions were focused on defining presence and impression, working on aspects that I could control including my temperament, comportment and verbal expression. I decided that I would speak, act and present in a consistent, professional manner. I worked to be well-spoken and confident even when under stress and I honed my

I coach others to be the leader they want to lead.

ability to command a room.

I coach others to be the leader they want to lead them rather than act immaturely and revert to negative behavior, e.g., become argumentative or dismissive. I urge them to call upon the positive aspects of compartmentalization – to set aside feelings and behaviors that are best when with family and friends and to actively employ a professional or public persona. This should be a purposeful process filled with tangible actions and being mindful of the intangible elements that have been incorporated. Consider it a discovery phase, asking yourself when am I at my most confident? Was it because I was prepared fully? Are there certain articles of clothing that shift my thinking to act more responsibly? Did I buy a piece of jewelry when I received a promotion that reminds me of my success every time I wear it?

After a client identifies what gives them confidence, pushes them to act maturely, and establishes the business mindset, I then ask about the actions and thoughts that diminish confidence and don't belong at work and actually create avoidable workplace challenges. Lastly, I begin a discussion about compartmentalization. This may entail reading and discussing articles on emotional intelligence as well as conducting a self-review. Realizing who you want to be as a professional is a vital undertaking for those who aspire being a more complete leader.

Chapter 10 Workbook

The Public You Versus the Private You

1. What are the main differences between the public you and the private you?

2. What do you do to move into your public persona? What do you do to transition from home to work and vice versa?

3. How will you use compartmentalization to maintain the idea that "this is business, don't take it personally?"

4. How have you consciously decided not to let others decide how successful you can be?

5. When are you the most confident? What did you do to achieve a high degree of confidence?

Chapter 11

If you think of something, do it.
Plenty of people often think,
"I'd like to do this, or that."

−Lydia Davis

Are You Your Own Worst Enemy?

Key chapter points

- Understand when you are your own worst enemy
- Identify virtual and real roadblocks to success
- Put an end to self-sabotage

I'm starting this chapter by sharing an internal conversation I have had with myself for some two decades.

A story:

Early in 2000 I said to myself, "I want to write a book. I need to write a book. I should write a book. But what do I have to say, who would read it? Just let it rest and mull on it." Sometime in 2002 I said, "OK, time to think about writing a book again. What would I write about? Who would read it? Well, just give it more time." In 2005 it was, "I NEED TO WRITE A BOOK. It is holding me back. I read the books others write on leadership and think I have valuable things to say on the subject. Why don't I think about that?"

This and similar versions went on in my head until 2020, the year of COVID-19 that changed much of my professional life. As a frequent flyer for some 25 years, I was proud of my two-million-mile status. (I wrote that statement and wondered exactly who I was to see that as an achievement!) Then, poof, there was no more air travel. I came home from a trip the last day of February 2020 and did not fly again until some 10 months later. Work as a leadership and strategy consultant quickly dried up, and there I was wondering what I could do to remain viable. And that's when I heard the long ignored, often repeated internal conversation about writing a book. This time I decided to put aside my fears and anxiety and actually do it. And now, two plus years later, you are reading my book.

So, what made me my own worst enemy? What created fear and doubt about my ability to add to the collective wisdom about leadership? The short answer is I ruminated about my doubts of being a writer. In my head, I created assumptions and scenarios that didn't but could exist. It was the COULD that held me back. It was better not to overreach, to be satisfied with what I have accomplished. Yet my whole career had been built on the overreach and not being satisfied. What I had done was become my own worst enemy, and rather than use the positive skills I had developed, I listened to a voice that lies deeply within most of us: Don't overstep. Know your limitations.

The realization of what I had done made me stop and think about those I coached. We all set up virtual and real roadblocks that only we can see and that may puzzle others. But it is our inability to believe in ourselves and act upon that belief that stops us from achieving. This inadvertent inaction creates doubt about our abilities so we don't move as confidently as we should even though we are capable of doing great things.

To identify areas of inaction you must dig beneath the surface. Where did my apprehension lie about putting my words in writing? What was the worst that could happen if I did write a book? I had to believe thoroughly in my ability to write, I had to trust myself and I had to let go of my fears and "just do it." I remind those I coach that the Nike slogan is invaluable advice when they discover they are creating barriers to their success. Sometimes it is enough to know YOU are causing the problem and it is time to get on with it.

Another aspect of being your own worst enemy is the act of sabotaging your advancement and success. The sabotage I refer to are deliberate acts akin to burning one's bridges before it is necessary. There are two types of deliberate acts: the first is airing our shortcomings before anyone notices them and second is not owning our success. As women we are accultured to own our errors or limitations before others notice them. In fact, to our detriment, we often bring them up, "Oh, I am not good at that" or "Before you ask, that is not a strong point for me." I have long thought of this as the antithesis of the Girl Scout badge sash. When I was a Girl Scout, we were encouraged to learn skills and when we did a badge was awarded as an accomplishment. Every badge earned was sewn onto a sash that we wore on top of our blouse from shoulder to hip. When I hear myself or other women bring up our issues before anyone else can point them out, I see it as earning a negative badge that we figuratively sew on our clothes.

In the second instance, too often women downplay recognition or praise when given and say, "Oh, anyone could do that!" or "What Annie or Sam did was far more important." We were taught not to think too highly of ourselves and continue to take it to heart by being dismissive of accolades. I encourage those I coach to accept praise with the same respect that they acknowledge their shortcomings. When I say this, the most common reaction is a pause and then for some almost an instant connection. For others, the very act I am referring to is so reflexive that their puzzlement turns into defensive statements about why they do it. As women, we need to learn to accept praise as well as our male colleagues and in doing so will avoid becoming our own enemy.

Accept praise with the same respect that you acknowledge your shortcomings.

Chapter 11 Workbook

Are You Your Own Worst Enemy?

1. Recall a situation when you were your own worst enemy. What delaying tactics did you use to avoid doing something? How did you convince yourself you were not capable?

2. Recall a situation where you readily stepped over your limitations. What enabled you to move forward, to make a change or just do it?

3. How do you own your success just as you own your shortcomings?

Chapter 12

*I never intended to become
a run of the mill person.*

–Barbara Jordan

Going Forward, It's Up to You

Key chapter points

- Decide, then do it
- Do regular confidence checkups
- Realize it is *your* book

Growing as a professional and a leader is an ongoing process. There is no end point. It is a continual work in progress. It ensures a sense of connection and action that makes us proud of what we accomplish and the very work we do. When we fall into a rut, life does become ordinary and like Barbara Jordan, I do not want to be ordinary. I challenge you not to be ordinary but to take up six calls to action:

- Be bold. Decide what you will do each day that is positive. Example: I choose to celebrate women as leaders every day. I choose to speak up when outdated thinking dominates the workplace. I seek inspiration from women and men who day after day seek to be the manager of their own book.

- Be determined. Decide what you will do each day that feeds your soul. Example: I will recognize my contributions. I will spend time each day on areas I love in my job. I will be kind to myself.

- Be realistic. Decide what obstacles are in the way of your success. Example: I will not defeat myself. I will ask more questions to gain greater understanding. I will let others know when a timeline can't be met and what I am doing about it. I will ask for help before I begin to drown.

- Be honest. Identify aspects of your job that are mundane but necessary. Example: I struggle doing XYZ because it's boring or beneath me or irksome. But when I make it about me, that impacts those around me. I will do more than be aware of my actions. I will do something about them.

- Be brave. The worst thing is to be silent when you or others are overlooked for a contribution. Figure out your mantra for being brave. Example: I will take a stand. I will always try. I will always be prepared. I will always care.

- Be confident and believe in yourself. Own the sense that "I can," "I am," I will," and "I belong." It is what pushes you through when your stomach is churning, your mind is blank, and the desire to flee is overwhelming.

That last bullet point, be confident and believe in yourself, should be a fundamental tenet of your emotional makeup. Just as you work on your tangible skill set, take time to assess your confidence capability. Understand when you are the most confident and when your confidence takes a holiday.

Review the circumstances: How did you prepare (or not)? Did you put your best foot forward or wing it? Were you focused on success or uncertainty? There are triggers that determine your level of confidence and can negatively or positively influence the way others hear, see and respond to you. Make a confidence checkup part of your preparation routine when faced with a challenge or an opportunity for advancement. It can be a difference maker.

My last story is an example of what I mistook for confidence as a less experienced supervisor.

The last story:

I was the manager of a restaurant in a four-diamond business and conference hotel in the Midwest. I was ill-prepared to direct an operation that served breakfast, lunch and dinner and was known locally for a great Sunday brunch. Breakfast was the busiest meal. Time was the major factor as no one wanted to wait for coffee and food – expediency was demanded. Scheduling was critical and reliability was the top priority, because if your crew did not show up on time problems just accumulated. In my infinite wisdom, I decided to change people's schedules with the thought it would be good for the crew to understand the differences between the day and night shift. I did not discuss this with the very capable and experienced host staff nor with my direct manager, the head of food and beverage. No, I wanted to do this on my own.

Well, the first morning of the new change was a disaster, with more than half of the guests receiving whatever they were served for no charge. The kitchen was in an uproar at the serving crew and my most reliable host was threatening to quit. Oh, and the general manager (GM) was livid over the number of complaints he received upon walking into the building. I went into work looking forward to a wonderful review by all, being appreciated for my initiative and hearing accolades from the crew.

What I found was a forest fire of complaints from the crew, the kitchen, my boss, the GM and the customers. But the biggest issue was the host who was recognized as the glue to the beginning of a good day in the hotel. In no uncertain terms I was told to fix the problem and to get the host to stay. My plan, my whole plan, was to say I'm sorry in a winsome way and that would be that. The host let me know in no uncertain terms being sorry did not cut it as it was clear I knew nothing about running a restaurant much less the breakfast shift. After much eating of humble pie on my part I did manage to retain the host, redid the schedule, and apologized to the chef, the crew and customers. I took a dressing down by my boss, as well as becoming the subject of discussion among my colleagues in the hotel.

From this incident, I learned the difference between hubris and confidence. We want to work with people who demonstrate consideration but make decisions. We want to work with people who have stumbled but got up and flew higher because of it. We want to work with people who have achieved and in return will provide us access, direction and resources to achieve. Your goal should be to become someone you want to work with.

Leadership is a subject I am passionate about. Some think passion is an unusual emotion to tie to the concept of leadership, but I believe it is often the missing element in our professional lives. Each of us displays passion differently but when transmitted consistently and with natural sensibility, the emotion becomes a clear demonstration of our commitment to colleagues and employees. Leadership is not about titles and position. It is about feelings, values and beliefs that create a desire in us to do better, to be a part of something that connects us, that spurs us on to do more, be more. Be the leader you want to work for.

Resolve that the book on you will be different: better, less or more of something going forward. There is no end point. Rather it is a work in progress. Persistent improvement is what great leaders are about, ensuring a sense of connection and action that makes us proud to be engaged with individuals and organizations. Being what you want in others is your goal.

I leave you with a quote from Carol Burnett, whom I have admired from afar for most of my life. She is multi-talented, does her job professionally with joy and humor, carries pain and disappointment with grace, and is far more than what most see her as. As you work to better who and what you are professionally, place Carol's belief at the forefront: *"Only I can change my life. No one can do it for me."*

This is your journey and so modify any idea you like within these chapters. Focus on what resonates with you. Go on a quest to elevate an aspect of your behavior or being. Never be defined by others. Always manage your own book.

Chapter 12 Workbook

Going Forward, It's Up to You

1. Take each of the six calls to action: be bold, be determined, be realistic, be honest, be brave, be confident and believe in yourself and decide how you will meet each challenge going forward.

I resolve to be bold. Here is how:

I resolve to be determined. Here is how:

I resolve to be realistic. Here is how:

I resolve to be honest. Here is how:

I resolve to be brave. Here is how:

I resolve to be confident and believe in myself. Here is how:

Assess your confidence capability.

1. Determine when you are the most confident and when your confidence takes a holiday.

2. Review the circumstances: How did you prepare (or not)? Did you put your best foot forward or wing it? Were you focused on success or uncertainty?

3. What will you do to become someone you want to work with? What will you do to become the leader you want?

Quoted Resources

Chapter 1: Time to Begin

Quote: "I don't see how (s)he can ever finish, if (s)he doesn't begin." Alice of *Alice in Wonderland*. A book written by English author Lewis Carroll in 1865.

Chapter 2: Knowing Yourself as a Professional

Quote: "Don't get confused between what people say you are and who you know you are." Oprah Winfrey. An American talk show host, television producer, actress and author.

Chapter 3: Knowing the View Others Have of You

Quote: "What we see depends mainly on what we look for." John Lubbock, The Beauties of Nature and the Wonders of the World We Live In. (Kirk, 2011), British banker, politician and naturalist.

Chapter 4: Owning Your First Impression

Quote: "Don't judge a book by its cover." Mr. Tulliver in the book *The Mill on the Floss* (1860) by George Eliot, the pen name of Mary Ann Evans. She was an English novelist, poet, journalist, translator and one of the leading writers of the Victorian era

To further you understanding bias and compartmentalization I suggest reading: Ross, Howard J. (2015, April 16). *3 Ways to Make Less Biased Decisions*. Harvard Business Review retrieved (June 2022), from https://hbr.org/2015/04/3-ways-to-make-less-biased-decisions?autocomplete=true

Chapter 5: Embrace Who You Are

Quote: "Be yourself, everyone else is already taken." Attributed to Oscar Wilde, Irish poet and playwright.

Chapter 6: Perspective Matters

Quote:" It's not only moving that creates new starting points. Sometimes all it takes is a subtle shift in perspective, an opening of the mind, an intentional pause and reset, or a new route to start to see new options and new possibilities." Kristin Armstrong. Professional road bicycle racer and three-time Olympic gold medalist.

Chapter 7: Choose to Be

Quote: "The greater danger for most of us lies not in setting our aim too high and falling short; but in setting our aim too low and achieving our mark." Michelangelo. Italian sculptor, painter, architect and poet of the High Renaissance.

Chapter 8:   Moving Beyond Fear of Failure

Quote: "Winning is great, sure, but if you are really going to do something in life, the secret is learning how to lose. Nobody goes undefeated all the time. If you can pick up after a crushing defeat, and go on to win again, you are going to be a champion someday." Wilma Rudolph. American sprinter, who became a world-record-holding Olympic champion and international sports icon in track and field following her successes in the 1956 and 1960 Olympic Games.

Quote: "Mistakes are a fact of life. It is the response to the error that counts." Nikki Giovanni. American poet, writer, commentator, activist and educator.

Chapter 9: Inspire Yourself and Others

Quote: "Our chief want is someone who will inspire us to be what we know we could be." Ralph Waldo Emerson. American essayist, lecturer, philosopher, abolitionist, and poet who led the transcendentalist movement of the mid-19th century.

Chapter 10: The Public You Versus the Private You

Quote: I'm a very private person, and when I leave the stage, I leave the stage." Helen Reddy. Australian-American singer, songwriter, author, actress, and activist.

Chapter 11. Are You Your Own Worst Enemy?

Quote: "If you think of something, do it. Plenty of people often think, 'I'd like to do this, or that.'"

Lydia Davis. Break It Down: Stories. Farrar, Straus and Giroux, 2008. American short story writer, novelist, essayist.

Chapter 12: Going Forward, It's Up to You

Quote: "I never intended to become a run-of-the-mill person." Barbara Jordan. American lawyer, educator, and politician who was a leader in the Civil Rights Movement.

Quote: "Only I can change my life. No one can do it for me." Carol Burnett. American actress, comedian, singer and writer.

About the Author

Lalia Rach is from Spring Green WI. While it took her longer than many to find her way in life, once she did it was full steam ahead!

Lalia's love of reading and thinking and her willingness to imagine grew into a determination to achieve beyond whatever confines attempted to surround her. She has traveled the world, experiencing many cultures and peoples. She has learned that what is the most important thing in life are the people you love. She has grown to be able to laugh at herself with regularity and has found joy in being. After 16 moves, she is back in her home state of Wisconsin enjoying being close to siblings, nieces and nephews, grandnieces and a grandnephew.

Index

Thank You for Finishing the Book

Before you go...

- Consider a review on Amazon.

- Tweet to your favorite people.

- Share on your favorite social media.

- Buy a copy for family, friends or clients in need.

- Let people know that I am open to helping at any time, email laliarach@rachenterprises.com or lalia@alhi.com

Reviews really are golden to writers. Please take a few minutes and write one now.

Notes